# Put Your Worries Here

A Creative Journal for
Teens with Anxiety

## Lisa M. Schab, LCSW

INSTANT HELP BOOKS

An Imprint of New Harbinger Publications, Inc.

## Publisher's Note

Distributed in Canada by Raincoast Books

Copyright © 2019 by Lisa Schab
               Instant Help Books
               An imprint of New Harbinger Publications, Inc.
               5674 Shattuck Avenue
               Oakland, CA 94609
               www.newharbinger.com

Cover and interior design by Amy Shoup

Acquired by Tesilya Hanauer

Library of Congress Cataloging-in-Publication Data
on file with publisher

ISBN: 978-1-68403-214-3

21     20     19

10    9    8    7    6    5    4    3    2    1

# In Praise of *Put Your Worries Here*

"Lisa Schab has a talent for connecting with teenagers, and has proven her expertise yet again. This creative journal is stocked with prompts for teens to identify their anxious thoughts, challenge their unhelpful thinking patterns, and learn new skills for managing anxiety symptoms. While the subtitle suggests this journal is for teens only, I am proof that you can be a thirty-six-year-old adult and find this creative journal both enjoyable and helpful!"

—MEGAN SAYRE, LCSW, adolescent psychotherapist in private practice, certified eating disorder specialist, and gender therapist

"In *Put Your Worries Here*, Lisa Schab helps teens tap into their senses with art, poetry, music, and writing to creatively develop a personalized set of anxiety-management skills. Founded in solid principles of psychotherapy practice, Schab has artfully created a space for teens to use journal prompts that guide them toward self-regulation. Even better, each teen will 'own it' as they actively participate in making this a book of their best ideas for calming the mind, the body, and behavior of anxiety. Put your worries about getting a good journal for teens right here."

—MARGARET WEHRENBERG, PsyD, anxiety coach for professionals, international trainer, and author of *The 10 Best-Ever Anxiety Management Techniques* and *Tough to Treat Anxiety*

"This book offers valuable, fun, creative, and simple activities that will help teens come into the present moment and retrain their anxious minds."

—JENNIFER SHANNON, LMFT, best-selling author of *The Anxiety Survival Guide for Teens* and *The Shyness and Social Anxiety Workbook for Teens*

"An engaging workbook from start to finish. Readers are encouraged to doodle, write, and reflect in response to the various friendly prompts. *Put Your Worries Here* is the book for anyone suffering from anxiety, and it promotes healthy messages of happiness and peace."
—JESSICA BURKHART, editor of *Life Inside My Mind*

"To change a behavior, you must have the will and the skill. Through a self-guided journey, Lisa Schab's *Put Your Worries Here* is an empowering tool that gives teens the skills to overcome anxiety. Rather than the 'experts' telling you what you should feel, each page helps you discard anxiety and lets you know that you are in control of your feelings. This book is a first step in getting control of your life."
—TOM WORTHEN, PhD, editor of *Broken Hearts Healing*, and adjunct professor at Utah State University

"*Put Your Worries Here* makes the perfect gift for anxious, stressed-out teens. It gently guides teens towards a myriad of anxiety-reduction strategies using lighthearted prompts that teens can change to suit their own needs. This journal is an inspired way to motivate anxious teens towards positive change!"
—SHEILA ACHAR JOSEPHS, PhD, speaker and consultant on managing anxiety in children and teens, and author of *Helping Your Anxious Teen*

"Practical, effective, and most of all, FUN, *Put Your Worries Here* will offer you dozens of ways to manage your anxiety through your greatest strength—your own creativity."
—CHRISTOPHER WILLARD, PsyD, faculty at Harvard Medical School, author of *Mindfulness for Teen Anxiety* and *Growing Up Mindful*, and coeditor of *Teaching Mindfulness Skills to Kids and Teens*

"I wished I'd had this journal when I was navigating adolescence. Filled with practical activities that speak to the modern teenager, it allows a personalized safe space to create a sense of peace. Imagine allowing your anxiety to escape through the holes in your jeans, or creating your own peace tattoo. Any teen living in the world today could utilize this book whether or not they have anxiety, and I will be recommending it to my patients."

—LISA K. DIAMOND, DNP, FNP-C, assistant professor of graduate nursing at the University of Colorado Anschutz Medical Campus, family nurse practitioner, and workshop developer of Journaling for Mindfulness and Stress Reduction

"Put Your Worries Here is an empowering, engaging, and wonderfully user-friendly journal designed to help teens struggling with anxiety to identify triggers which cause stress and discomfort, to learn effective self-soothing and coping skills, and to redirect energy toward building healthy self-esteem."

—JOAN MERLO, LCSW, psychotherapist in private practice with children, teens, and adults in Highland Park, IL; and staff therapist at Family Service of Glencoe in Glencoe, IL

"This creative journal encourages teens to explore their anxiety and identify strategies for coping with stress. Using creative writing and drawing exercises, readers can challenge the thinking and imagery that contribute to their anxiety. The creative exercises in this book are both engaging and unlike those that I have seen in other books on this topic. Yet, they are informed by standard, evidence-based treatments that are often used to help teens move from a state of anxiety to one of relaxation and calm. This book is ideal for the teen who is looking for a more creative approach to deal with anxiety and worry."

—MARTIN M. ANTONY, PhD, professor in the department of psychology at Ryerson University; author, coauthor, and editor of numerous titles, including The Shyness and Social Anxiety Workbook, The Anti-Anxiety Workbook, Oxford Handbook of Anxiety & Related Disorders, and more

To L.P.P.
who saved herself
in journals

and L.P.N.
who gave her
the first chance

START HERE

# First, some good things to know about anxiety:

**1.** **It's very common!** (Which means you're not the only one who feels it.)

## It's normal for teens to feel anxious about:

| | | |
|---|---|---|
| SCHOOL | LACK OF TIME | BODY IMAGE |
| FRIENDS | SADNESS | LOVE |
| PARENTS | SAFETY | GRADES |
| PEER PRESSURE | FAMILY PROBLEMS | GENDER ISSUES |
| APPEARANCE | | EMOTIONS |
| DATING | HOMEWORK | SEX |
| ANGER | FITTING IN | THE FUTURE |
| RELATIONSHIPS | COPING WITH STRESS | WHAT OTHERS THINK OF YOU |
| TESTS | ACHIEVEMENT | HEALTH |
| DRUGS AND ALCOHOL | EXPECTATIONS | . . . AND MORE |

### (Circle the ones you relate to.)

In fact, anxiety is the most common of all emotional problems.

**2.** **It's really treatable.** Anxiety doesn't have to run your life! There are so many ways to get a grip on it—and they're things the average teen can do.

## 3. Your brain's anxiety habit can be changed.

Whenever you choose peaceful thoughts over anxious ones, your brain cell pathways grow stronger for peace and weaker for anxiety. Even if you're not in a peaceful situation, just imagining you are helps your brain make this change. (This book gives you many ways to practice this.)

**Do you have any of these common anxiety symptoms?**
Circle the ones you'd like to reduce by using this journal:

worry

sweating

chills

racing heart

blushing

dizziness

shaking

nausea

muscle tension

fear

heart pounding

lightheadedness

sleep problems

belching

trouble breathing

low energy

trouble focusing

trouble speaking

chest pressure

digestion problems

chest tightness

headaches

feeling overwhelmed

feeling of dread

feeling of being "disconnected"

tiredness

chest pain

yawning

coughing

hyper-ventilating

Or . . .

_____

_____

_____

_____

_____

_____

# Second, some info about this book:

* **It's filled with "prompts"**—or suggestions—for activities that can help you release some anxiety and start changing your brain patterns right now.

* **It's yours to do in your way.** So you can do exactly what a prompt suggests, or you can do something that feels better for you. (For example, if it doesn't say "make stars around the edge of the page," you can still make stars around the edge of the page. If it suggests you color, you could write instead.) If it offers either too much or too little guidance, you can just respond however you like. Feel free to staple, glue, cut, paint, or add souvenirs and tokens from your life. Also, you can do these prompts in the order they appear, or in any order you like. **\*Be guided by what feels peaceful to you.\***

* **It's not English class.** You can use correct grammar, spelling, and punctuation, but it's not required.

* **It's not art class.** The suggestion "Draw" just means to put something on the paper using line and form—however that works for you.

**IMPORTANT NOTE:** The purpose of this book is to help you lower your anxiety. If a prompt raises your anxiety, just notice that and then move on. You may or may not want to revisit it at another time. You decide.

* If you really like a prompt, you can do it again— or as many times as you want. Use more paper if you need it.

* **There's no wrong way to do anything in here.** The goal is to just release some anxiety or shift your mind from anxiety to peace and calm. So, how you feel is more important than what you end up with. Try not to judge what happens on the paper.

* If any of the above ideas help you feel calm, circle, star, check, underline, highlight, or identify them in some way.

* If any of them raise your anxiety, try letting it out in this space:

* Add your own guidelines for using this book:

_____

_____

_____

_____

Write one peaceful, positive, or happy
thought . . . and take one quiet breath . . .
for each letter.

A

B

C

D

E

F

G

H

I

J

K

L

M

N

O

P

Q

R

S

T

U

V

W

X

Y

Z

Write your ⋮ anxious ⋮ thoughts on these pages.

Cover them with duct tape!

Tape or draw a picture of a peaceful place you love here.

Close your eyes and
visualize yourself there now.

This is your
ANXIETY FREE ZONE

What's in it?

"ANXIETY IS ONE LITTLE TREE IN YOUR FOREST. STEP BACK AND LOOK AT THE WHOLE FOREST."

—Author Unknown

calm

free

serene

relax

let go

slow down

chill

still

cleanse

breathe

peace

rest

pause

tranquil

ease

loose

release

unwind

silence

quiet

# Drink something warm and soothing.

## Write a thank you note from your body to you.

Dear _____,

Love, Your Body

# "Breathing in, I am calm;

Write it:

cursive

upside down

backward

in a different language

## as large as possible

as small as possible

**bold letters**

running off the page

nospacesbetweenwords

quiet letters

ALL CAPS

backward slant

*forward slant*

childish scrawl

alien alphabet

breathing out, I am peace."

Create a playlist of songs that help you de-stress. Write the best lyrics here.

21

Breathe peacefully . . .

and randomly connect the dots.

You're carrying a backpack filled with everything you need to stay calm.

What's in
each pocket?

25

# All the things that are going RIGHT today.

(Include everything. Did you wake up? Can you breathe?)

!  _____

   _____

!  _____

   _____

!  _____

   _____

!  _____

   _____

!  _____

   _____

!  _____

   _____

!  _____

   _____

!  _____

Draw a peace garden.

# Anxiety First Aid:

1. Run a stream of **cool water** down the inside of your forearms.

2. Wrap yourself up in a **hug**.

3. Trace soft, **slow circles** over the top of each knee with your fingertips.

4.

5.

6.

7.

8.

9.

10.

Add more ideas.

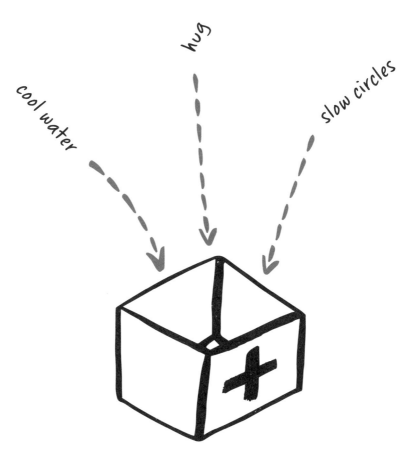

cool water

hug

slow circles

List the TOP THREE things you feel anxious about.

1.

2.

3.

Write about one until you have nothing left to say.

Close this book and move on.

Design your personal
anxiety-release button.

Slowly count to three.
Push the button.

# I am grateful for...

**People**

**Places**

# Things

___

# Break up with your anxiety.

Dear Anxiety,

Write it a Dear John letter.

Create a collage
using anything that brings you peace...

"I AM ABLE TO CLOSE
MY EYES AND GENERATE
THE FEELING OF TOTAL
PEACE ANYWHERE
AND ANYTIME."

—Mary Maddox

Write an anxious thought
in this square.

Cut it out and tape it to
the bottom of your shoe.

**Grind it into the floor.**

FILL THIS PAGE WITH A PEACEFUL COLOR.

Design a peace tattoo.

Where would you put it?

# Your Best

Recreate it—or create it—here.

Day Ever.

Your anxiety just texted you AGAIN.

Write your responses and remind it that you're the boss.

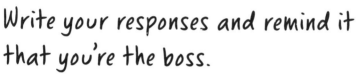

51

Let someone you trust gently rub your back.

What happens in your body, mind and spirit?

# Start a collection here of . . .

funny lines

jokes

memes

quotes

sayings

links

or anything else that makes you
laugh out loud.

The universe is speaking calming
thoughts to you.

What is it saying?

# How are you different?

YOU

# YOUR ANXIETY

Find a photo or two

that make you smile.

Tape them here.

Decorate the surrounding space.

You are babysitting an anxious child. Write the story—fact or fiction—that would calm them down and help them sleep.

_____
_____
_____
_____
_____
_____
_____
_____
_____
_____
_____
_____
_____
_____
_____

AFFIRM out loud ... BELIEVE in your mind ...
FEEL in your body ...

# "I am the most

## on the face of

peaceful person

the earth."

What is it like?

Write your anxious thoughts that include words like "never," "always," "everyone," or "no one."


ALWAYS




NO ONE

NEVER

EVERYONE

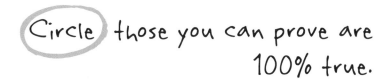 those you can prove are 100% true.

Take a walk outdoors.

Preserve something from nature here.

You fired your anxiety, effective today.
Write its termination letter.

↓

(What's in the box it takes when it leaves your body and mind?)

Draw and describe the bridge that will take you from anxiety to peace.

# Present moment details:

today's date

the hour

the season

two things you hear

1.

2.

the taste in your mouth

six things you see

1.

2.                                    the weather

3.

4.

5.

6.


a texture you feel on your body



any fragrance in the air



something that makes you smile

Draw an outline of your brain.
Put peaceful words and thoughts inside.

Your anxiety has just escaped through the rips in your jeans. **It's gone for good!**

What is life like now?

# What are you like?

Some people say . . .

"There's a reason for everything."

"This, too, shall pass."

"My struggle today is my strength tomorrow."

What words help you?

Write your favorites . . . or create your own.

"THE BRAVE MAN IS NOT HE WHO DOES NOT FEEL AFRAID, BUT HE WHO CONQUERS THAT FEAR."

—Nelson Mandela

What thoughts keep you in anxiety prison? Write them on the bars. Then tear them up and break free.

Draw a peaceful cloud floating in the sky. Write your name on it.

You are
a peace
magnet.

What are
you attracting
to yourself
right now?

How would you help your
best friend calm down?

Do this for yourself now.

# What anxious thoughts are floating

List them under the correct headings.

**FACTS:** Statements that can be proven true and correct no matter what. ("I am human.")

FEELINGS: Statements that may feel very true but are actually matters of opinion and could be disputed. ("I am a terrible artist.")

# Decorate the night sky.
## Then, touch a star for each number as you count and breathe:

inhale to the count of 2, exhale to 2 —

inhale to 2, exhale to 4 —

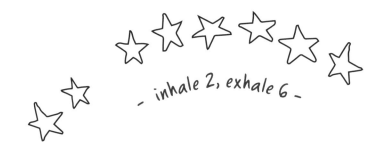

- inhale 2, exhale 6 -

- inhale 2, exhale 8 -

- inhale 2, exhale 10 -

Repeat until you feel relaxed.

## Describe the five best things
### that ever happened to you.

1.

2.

3.

4.

5.

# CLEAN OUT

# THE ANXIETY CLOSET

# OF YOUR MIND.

PUT YOUR UNWANTED

THOUGHTS IN THE

TRASH CONTAINER,

THEN MARK OVER IT UNTIL

THEY DISAPPEAR.

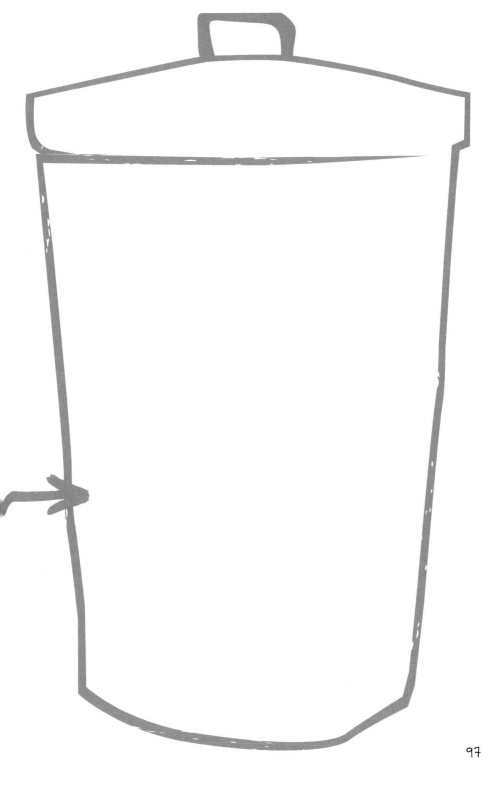

Your superpower is Calm.


Your superhero name:

_____

_____


What you look like:

How you defeat anxiety:

What are you afraid to say out loud?
Draw a safe space and write it here.

Take a breath.

# Doodle peace.

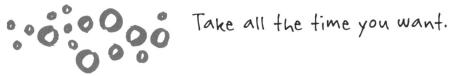
Take all the time you want.

Ask someone you trust to write
you a comforting message.

Tape or copy it here.

# Circle the words that bring you peace:

| | | | |
|---|---|---|---|
| sand | numbers | morning | snow |
| water | sleep | lake | play |
| spring | dark | together | evening |
| autumn | ocean | cool | summer |
| warm | light | alone | desert |
| winter | letters | arts | forest |

Use any of these—or others—to create
word pictures or lines of a poem.

Gaze at something
peaceful for
five minutes.
When your mind
wanders, smile,
and gently
bring it back.

Write or draw when you're done.

"WHEN EATING AN
ELEPHANT, TAKE ONE
BITE AT A TIME."

—General Creighton W. Abrams

# What's overwhelming you?
Break it down into smaller steps and
write them in the shapes.

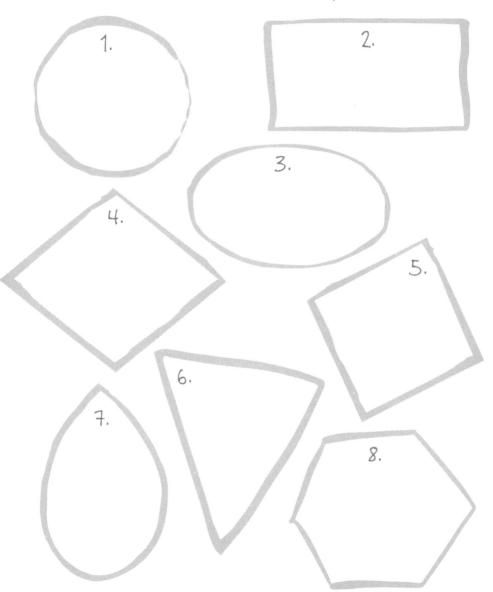

1.

2.

3.

4.

5.

6.

7.

8.

# Five

# minute

# dance

# break!

How do you feel now?

# ☀ Things I can't change ☀
## (I accept them and let them go.)

# ✳ Things I can change ✳
## (I have the courage to try!)

What relaxing view would you like to

Identify the "should" thoughts that make you feel guilty or be too hard on yourself. Then rewrite them with a voice of caring and compassion.

I should ...

119

# Trace your toes here.
## Give each one a name.

Left

Draw smiles on them—or hats—
or bow ties—or?

Right

Calm breath . . .
comfy chair . . .
Write by candle light.

"I'm steady and strong."

"I am well."

"I am centered in peace."

Breathe quietly, and write more calming affirmations for your mind and body.

Design a license plate for the

# State of Tranquility.

Include a state motto.

# You're having an argument with your anxiety. **You win.**

You are walking in a gentle rain and it rinses off all your anxiety.

What's left?

"I'M FRIGHTENED ALL THE TIME. SCARED TO DEATH. BUT I'VE NEVER LET IT STOP ME. NEVER!"

—Georgia O'Keeffe

# LIST YOUR ANXIOUS THOUGHTS.

_____

_____

_____

_____

_____

_____

_____

_____

_____

_____

_____

_____

_____

_____

_____

_____

_____

_____

_____

_____

## THEN TEAR OUT THIS PAGE AND SHRED IT.

Leave this page blank.

Take a breath.

Just be.

Draw or tape a picture of your
Peace House here.

What is your room like?
What would it be like to live here?

Fill each
QUILT SQUARE
with

something
that
makes you

feel peaceful,
positive, calm.

Your anxiety is on a bus to Nowhere.
What thoughts are in the seats?

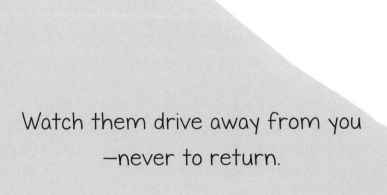

Watch them drive away from you
—never to return.

What do you wear to feel cozy
and relaxed?

Put on your comfy clothes and fill these

pages with whatever feels good right now. ～

# WHO'S THE MOST PEACEFUL PERSON YOU KNOW?

### PHOTO HERE.

# WHAT ARE THEY LIKE?

* _____

_____

* _____

_____

* _____

_____

* _____

_____

* _____

_____

* _____

_____

* _____

* _____

Use lines, shapes, and textures to let out your anxiety.

Fill these pages.

Imagine you're
the best parent in the world.
How would you care for yourself
right now?

Do it.

Write while in, on, or looking

Find the stillness

at a body of water.

beneath the surface.

Draw
    drifting
       feathers

or tape real feathers across these pages.

Fill and surround them with
peaceful words, images, colors.

DO SOMETHING GOOFY OR RIDICULOUS
ON OR TO THESE PAGES.

154

NO RULES-

EXCEPT THAT IT MAKES YOU LAUGH!

Add words or pictures to the phrases
that bring you peace . . .

> mountain lake

> deep forest

> sunset

> ocean waves

> dawn's first light

> green meadow

 Or—?

Your mind's voice mailbox is full of
**anxiety-causing messages**
from both yourself and others.

List the messages you want to delete.

1. _____
   _____
   _____

2. _____
   _____
   _____

3. _____
   _____
   _____

4. _____
   _____
   _____

5. _____

_____

_____

_____

6. _____

_____

_____

_____

7. _____

_____

_____

_____

8. _____

_____

_____

_____

9. _____

_____

_____

_____

Do it.

"YOU CAN'T STOP THE WAVES BUT YOU CAN LEARN HOW TO SURF."

—Jon Kabat-Zinn

Touch a drop of vanilla—
or lavender—or another
calming essential oil
across this page.

Breathe in . . . breathe out.

What would you be doing right now if you weren't feeling anxious?

Now close this book and do it.

Quiet your body.

Breathe.

Clear your mind.

Listen.

Be still.

Feel.

What do you notice?

Take charge of your big fears
by making them small words
or pictures on these pages.

Tape something bigger over them.

PLAY MUSIC THAT RELAXES YOU.

FILL THESE PAGES WHILE YOU LISTEN.

Take this book somewhere you
feel comfortable and safe.

What makes this place good?

Warm hoodie.

Fluffy stuffy.

Silky dog ears.

Fleecy blanket.

What **calms** you
when you touch it?

Put a picture of it here.

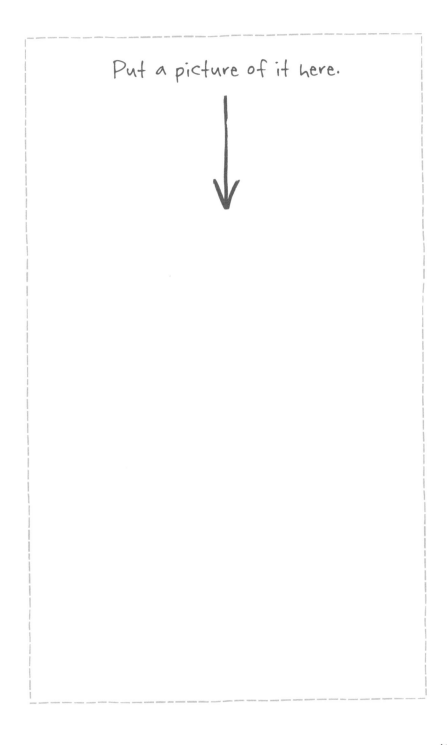

List any situations where you feel
little or no anxiety.

* _____

_____

_____

* _____

_____

_____

* _____

_____

_____

* _____

_____

_____

* _____

_____

*  _____

   _____

   _____

*  _____

   _____

   _____

*  _____

   _____

   _____

*  _____

   _____

   _____

*  _____

   _____

Replay one ⌐or more in your mind and your body.

Put images of flying birds here.
Write an anxious thought in each one.

Let them fly by.

CLOSE
YOUR EYES
AND
BREATHE
PEACEFULLY.

Imagine
a soft,
warm
golden
light
flowing
gently
through
your
entire
body
from
head to
toe.

Draw your peace-filled self.

# It's early morning.

List the thoughts you feed your brain to make your whole day peaceful.

_____

_____

_____

_____

_____

_____

_____

_____

_____

_____

_____

_____

_____

_____

# Find a playground.
Climb, swing, slide, or do whatever
frees your spirit. Then fill these pages.

This crystal ball shows your peaceful future.

Fill it with everything
that will be better
one year from today.

# WHAT TO DO NEXT

**When you've completed all the prompts you want to,** take a look at what you've got now: a whole book filled with your "empowerment" (the process of becoming stronger and more confident). You've just created a physical representation of your ability to manage anxiety. This journal is proof that you are not a victim, you have choices, and you can affect the tension level in your body and the thoughts that enter your mind. You aren't stuck feeling anxious forever.

**Your journal is now a valuable tool.** It's a concrete reminder of your strength, and it's filled with information about ways to help yourself release some anxiety. And, you can keep using it to do that. You might want to keep it in your backpack, under your bed, or in some other easily reachable place to pull out when you need it. You can also try these ideas . . .

When you're feeling anxious, go through this book and add peaceful colors, words, or designs in any place and in any way that feels good to you.

Fill this page, too.

Make copies or take pictures of the pages that help you feel the most peaceful or powerful. Put them on your mirror, in your locker, on your phone, or anywhere else you'll see them and be inspired.

WRITE YOUR TOP 3 FAVORITES HERE:

1.

2.

3.

# MAKE LISTS OF
# THE PROMPTS THAT HELP:

RELAX MY BODY

REMIND ME
I'M STRONGER
THAN ANXIETY

INCREASE MY PEACE

MAKE ME SMILE

SHIFT MY THOUGHTS
AWAY FROM ANXIETY

Make a peace pizza.

Go back through this book and choose
the words and images you'd
like for your toppings.
Recreate them on
this crust.

Write your own prompt here:

## Note to parents, professionals, and anyone caring for an anxious teen:

Anxiety is a feeling of unease or nervousness in the mind and/or body evoked by situational or chemical elements that produce thoughts of worry or fear.

*Put Your Worries Here* offers 100 journaling prompts designed specifically to help teens manage and release anxiety in the moment. Creative, engaging, and clinically based, all prompts are grounded in principles of Cognitive Behavioral Therapy, Dialectical Behavioral Therapy, mindfulness-based therapies, experiential therapies, or neuroscience.

The journal can be used by a teen on their own, or as an adjunct to counseling or psychotherapy. It lends itself both to individual and group settings and can help the average adolescent as well as the hard-to-reach teen and those uncomfortable with traditional talk therapy.

Where direct questioning and exploration might feel threatening, journaling prompts are more subtle and can bypass defenses. When used at times of stress, the journal can interrupt the anxiety cycle and help relieve physical and emotional symptoms. Prompts are designed to change unhealthy thinking and breathing patterns, release physical tension, increase endorphin flow, strengthen neural pathways for peace, and empower the anxious teen. Creative prompts can help teens identify anxiety triggers, develop coping skills, and regulate emotion while still maintaining comfort with the process.

For a clinician's guide to using this book specifically, and journaling as an adjunct to therapy in general, please visit http://www.lisamschabooks.com. There you'll also find a guide for parents. Alternatively, you can visit http://www.newharbinger.com/42143 and follow the instructions there to register your book and download the companion guides. If you are interested in earning continuing education credits for Lisa Schab's courses on journaling as an adjunct to therapy, please visit https://www.pdresources.org/.

# Acknowledgments

I would like to thank:

Tesilya – as always, for the initial opportunity and so much patience

Clancy – for continued cheerleading and awesome input

Amy S., Michele, and Sara – for the phenomenal visuals that breathed life into these pages

Amy B. – for more tracking and hunting!

The entire NHP sales and marketing team for working around my low-techness

The Creative Space that is so much bigger than my brain – for letting me tap in yet again

Lisa M. Schab, LCSW, is a licensed clinical social worker with a private counseling practice in the greater Chicago, IL, area. She has authored seventeen self-help books and workbooks for children, teens, and adults, including *The Anxiety Workbook for Teens* and *The Self-Esteem Workbook for Teens*. Schab teaches self-help workshops and professional training courses on both anxiety and journaling, and is a member of the National Association of Social Workers (NASW). You can find out more about her at www.lisamschabooks.com.